31
TRUTHS
TO SHAPE YOUR
YOUTH MINISTRY

Richard Ross

with

Patrick Janson, Michael Kelly, Yoojin Kim,
Jonathan Williams, and Clement Woo

Devotionals for all adults who love and value teenagers

SEMINARY HILL
PRESS

TABLE OF CONTENTS

START HERE . . .

How will you read this book?
　Consider reading a chapter a day for 31 days.
　Then set the book aside for a season.
　And then consider reading a chapter a day for another 31 days.

Why such a plan? A bottle of vitamins might contain lots of things your body needs. But if you consume the entire bottle at one time, your body will only have time to absorb a fraction of those good things. Consider this book that bottle of vitamins.

After King Jesus and my family, the great love of my life is teenagers. Not teenagers in the abstract, but living, breathing teenagers. They are on my mind when I wake up and when I go to bed. That has been true for more than 40 years.

I hunger to see teenagers who, for the glory of the Father and in the power of the Spirit, spend a lifetime embracing the full supremacy of the Son, responding to His majesty in all of life, inviting Christ to live His life through them, and joining Him in making disciples among all peoples.

I am keenly aware that the Almighty channels much Kingdom impact through significant adults in the lives of teenagers. Those adults include youth leaders, parents, youth pastors, and members of the congregation who love and value teenagers. I have designed this book for each of those adults. For simplicity, I will use the expression "youth leader" throughout the book to refer to *all* of those influencers.

May I Meet You Tomorrow?

Early every morning, I post a message on social media. Usually, the message is designed specifically for those who love and care for teenagers. The posts are public, so you don't need social media accounts to see them. I would love to connect with you each morning. Facebook.com/rossrichard, Twitter.com/richardaross

Other Books

This book mostly is designed for the heart. But I have written other books that go into much more detail concerning the philosophy, design, and implementation of youth ministry. The principles apply to churches of all sizes. Go to RichardARoss.com for full information about those books.

Partners in Writing

I am grateful to Patrick Janson, Michael Kelly, Yoojin Kim, Jonathan Williams, and Clement Woo for their partnership on this book. These Ph.D. students at Southwestern Seminary provided background research, Scripture study, and sections of text. These are gifted adults making an impact for the Kingdom, and I am honored to walk beside them.

List Below the Dates You Complete Reading This Book

TRUTH 1

Youth leaders magnify the greatness of King Jesus in the power of the Spirit for the glory of God.

Those who study church teenagers suggest that the following lines describe the "faith" of the majority: "Jesus came into the world for *me*. He will always be there for *me*, ensuring maximum happiness for *me*, and fulfilling all that concerns *me*."

Those same studies also suggest that teenagers have absorbed a me-centered faith from the important adults in their lives. I am a youth leader and a dad, so I must ask myself, "Do I value Jesus mostly for the advantages He brings to me?"

In 2006, God brought David Bryant into my life, and he began to illuminate the Scriptures that unfold the present glory of King Jesus. In my mind's eye, I was transported to heaven 40 days after the resurrection. I arrived just in time to hear the Father say to His returning Son,

"Sit at My right hand until I make
Your enemies a footstool for Your feet" (Psalm 110:1).

As Jesus was enthroned, I imagined myself joining myriads of angels and the redeemed of the ages in awe of His incomparable worthiness. We all lifted lofty worship before God's face; regaling Messiah's resounding, relentless, righteous, redeeming rule; celebrating the cosmic Champion who is anointed and active, decisive and invasive, unavoidable and unimpeachable, irresistible and irreplaceable.

Then, in my mind's eye, I traveled to the moment of Christ's second coming. As He split open the heavens and descended to earth, I was almost overwhelmed with His power and shimmering glory.

3

Then it dawned on me that what Jesus will be Lord of on that day He is Lord of on *this* day. All the glory He will display on that day is the glory that belongs to Him on *this* day.

I saw Jesus as I had never seen Him before! I felt as though the Father reintroduced me to His Son, as if I were meeting Jesus again for the very first time!

I have not been the same since.

This entire chapter is composed mostly of David's words that the Spirit continues to use to deepen my experience with King Jesus. David's newest book, *Christ Is Now!*, amplifies and enriches every sentence found here.[1]

What you think (and can share) about God's Son is the single most important thing anyone can know about you. Nothing about you as a youth leader matters more.

Which seems more valuable to you—the *centrality* of Christ or the *supremacy* of Christ? The *centrality* of Christ defines Him in terms of His role at the center of my life—who I am, where I am headed, what I am doing, and how I get blessed. The *supremacy* of Christ expresses His right to keep me at the center of His life—who He is, where He is headed, what He is doing, and how He is blessed.

Before awakening to the greatness of Jesus, I focus on getting Jesus to come to *me* to make my life better. But as I begin to embrace His majesty, I focus on going to *Him* so that I can become part of who He is and what He is doing.

Within the Trinity, the Father is so passionate for the Son that He has decreed that, in everything, the Son is to have the preeminence, the primacy, and the supremacy (Colossians 1).

Should Jesus be any less to us than the consuming passion of our lives?

Should Jesus be any less to our teenagers than the consuming passion of their lives?

Can any of our goals be fully realized unless the teenagers grasp who King Jesus really is?

What could be more important than a Christ-awakening in our youth group?

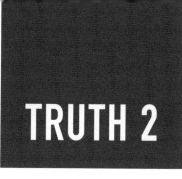

TRUTH 2

Youth leaders are called by God, empowered by the Spirit, and serve for the glory of King Jesus.

Only one reason is valid for entering ministry to and with teenagers: the inescapable conclusion that God has called you to do so. Other reasons for entering this ministry may be sincere, but they are inadequate. Among those other reasons may be:

1. You get to spend all your time running around with teenagers.
Time spent directly with teenagers is an exciting part of youth ministry, but it is only a part. Wise youth leaders today invest time with parents, recognizing that those parents will have the greatest spiritual impact on their teenagers—for good or ill. Also, youth leaders invest time with other adults on the youth ministry team. They depend on the team for mutual prayer support, ministry insights, and grace-filled accountability.

2. Youth leaders get to do wild, creative things all the time.
Youth ministry certainly has its moments of celebration and creativity. But such occasions are just the tip of the iceberg. Youth leaders invest much more time mining the riches of God's Word so they can teach, sharing coffee with a discouraged teenager or parent, laying out plans, and scores of other things that lead to lifetime ministry impact.

3. I count on teenagers to make me feel good about myself.
Youth leaders need to have an identity grounded in who they are in Christ. (See Truth 10 for more insights about grounding your identity in Christ alone.) Adults who want to have their needs met by teenagers or by the status of being a leader need more discipleship

and healing before they enter youth ministry. The same is true for leaders who cling to teenagers as a way to avoid adult relationships.

Again, the only valid reason for entering youth ministry is the inescapable conclusion that God has called you to do so. God calls out leaders today just as He called out Moses and Paul. He may not use a burning bush or a flash of light, but His call is just as real. Potential leaders seeking to know His will might ask:

1. Generally, do I have a walk with Christ that is alive and growing?
2. Do I draw from Scripture all I teach, counsel, and plan?
3. Do I have the capacity to offer unconditional love to teenagers that is warm and unselfish?
4. Will background checks reveal I am safe and trustworthy in all my relationships?
5. Do my spiritual leaders see in me the potential to serve in youth ministry?
6. When I pray deeply and pour over Scripture, do I sense direction from the Spirit to serve in youth ministry?
7. Do I long to have the Holy Spirit flowing through me into the lives of teenagers and their families, doing far more than is humanly possible?
8. In my heart of hearts, do I want to see teenagers spend a lifetime bringing great glory to King Jesus? Do I long to hear young voices say:

We behold you and rejoice in you as the triumphant Lamb before whom all creation and all the redeemed of all the ages bow down and worship, before whom all of us here and now bow down and worship.
To you belong blessing and honor and glory and strength and power forever and ever. All of Scripture, all of creation, all of history, all of the purposes and prophecies and promises of God are summed up *in you alone*.[2]

TRUTH 3

Youth leaders model what they desire teenagers to do and to be.

Youth ministry develops teenagers who increasingly become like Christ, thinking His thoughts, sharing His worldview, taking His Gospel to the world, and demonstrating His sacrificial compassion. All of that happens by the power of the Holy Spirit.

One of the Spirit's favorite tools for accomplishing this is youth leaders who increasingly become like Christ, thinking His thoughts, sharing His worldview, taking His Gospel to the world, and demonstrating His sacrificial compassion.

The old saying, "You can't lead folk where you haven't been," has an element of truth in it. The Christian life is caught as well as taught. That is why youth leaders model what they desire teenagers to do and to be.

God inspired the writer of Hebrews to say, "Remember those who led you, who spoke the word of God to you; and considering the result of their conduct, imitate their faith" (Hebrews 13:7). That leads every youth leader to ask:

"If our teenagers imitate me, will they then be more like Jesus?"

Christ is the perfect example for youth leaders. To be models for teenagers, youth leaders first must imitate Jesus. Peter said, "For you have been called for this purpose, since Christ also suffered for you, leaving you an example for you to follow in His steps" (1 Peter 2:21). Here, "example" means "to trace over" alphabet letters to correctly understand the letters. To be a good model for teenagers, youth leaders should trace over Christ's pattern in all they say and do.

Paul instructed young adult Timothy to set a good example for the church, writing, "Let no one look down on your youthfulness, but rather in speech, conduct, love, faith and purity, show yourself an example of those who believe" (1 Timothy 4:12).

When youth leaders teach teenagers, they present two lessons. One lesson is the biblical material they have prepared. The other lesson is who they are—hopefully, a high-definition illustration of the biblical truth they are teaching.

Youth leaders teach teenagers how to go deep in Christ. Leaders just need to take those steps themselves. They need to:

1. *Study the Bible apart from any teaching duties.*

Youth leaders need to do what they guide teenagers to do. They need to explore God's Word for personal inspiration and instruction. They need to experiment with various Bible study approaches and to record specific insights and applications that the Spirit gives them.

2. *Pray.*

A close walk with God without private prayer is as likely as a romance without conversation. Praying with the youth group and the entire church is important, but it cannot take the place of private prayer.

The great enemy of time in prayer is busyness. The answer is to have a daily quiet time early in the morning before hectic schedules begin.

3. *Find someone to walk beside you.*

Leaders need someone with whom they can share moral struggles and impending decisions. And it helps to know someone will be asking about the consistency of your time in the throne room with King Jesus. All of this leads youth leaders to adore Christ and abide in Him moment by moment.

> We should exhibit an "undying love" for him (Ephesians 6:24, NIV), even unto our own death (John 23; Revelation 12)—a love that drives us to eliminate everything in our lives incompatible with making Jesus our one and only "magnificent obsession" (Philippians 3).[3]

TRUTH 4

Youth leaders spiritually impact parents so that parents can spiritually impact their children.

Scripture teaches that parents are in the first position related to spiritual impact on their children: "You shall teach [God's commandments] diligently to your sons and shall talk of them when you sit in your house and when you walk by the way and when you lie down and when you rise up" (Deuteronomy 6:7).

Most children and teenagers reared by Christ-adoring parents become Christ-adoring young adults. Most children and teenagers reared by parents without Christ become young adults without Christ.

Surprisingly, most children and teenagers reared in spiritually shallow homes walk away from the faith altogether as young adults. Watching parents who attend church but do not fully embrace Christ and His Kingdom confuses them and even turns them against the faith.

Parents awaking to the supremacy of Jesus, parents more deeply adoring Him on His throne, and parents daily arising to join Him in His Kingdom activity offer the brightest hope for teenagers moving in those same directions. Therefore, youth leaders who want to see teenagers alive in Christ commit some of their time to parents.

The goal of investing in parents is not families sitting on the couch singing "Kumbaya." The end goal is families making disciples, locally and globally, for the glory of God. Spiritual practices in the home and more transformed family members are valuable because they prepare the saints for Kingdom service.

Through concerted prayers, informal conversations, and church gatherings, youth leaders spiritually pour into parents. Leaders develop parents who say, "I would love to see my teenager, for the glory of the Father and in the power of the Spirit, spend a lifetime embracing

9

the full majesty of Christ, become more and more like Him, and join Him in making disciples among all people."

To that end, youth leaders can make the following statements to parents:

1. Affirm God's call on your own life.

God placed you here because He deeply desires to have a relationship with you. You are here to share ever-increasing love, closeness, and fellowship with God, even as your awe of His holiness also deepens. Christ's supremacy within God's purposes will always be paired with His intimacy within parents and all of God's people.

Flowing out of that purpose, join Him in bringing His Kingdom on earth. You are called and gifted to love all people, introduce them to God through Christ, and then disciple them. Doing so brings glory to the Son of God, whom you love with all your heart.

2. Affirm God's call as a parent.

You and your spouse are called to lead your children to God through Christ and then disciple and lead them to join Him in bringing His Kingdom on earth. Any other assignment you have on earth pales in comparison to that one.

You are the most important spiritual leader of your children. You have more spiritual influence in their lives than any minister or church leader. You have to decide if that is good news or bad news.

3. Understand and put God's parenting essentials into practice.

Your love relationship with God and your discipleship journey will provide a powerful example—positive or negative—of what it means to be a Christian man or woman.

If you are spiritually alive and transparent, have strong heart connections with your children, and teach them God's truth, then they likely will spend a lifetime embracing the supreme majesty of Christ and living on mission with Him.

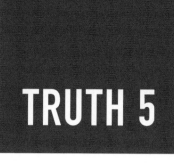

TRUTH 5

Youth leaders call out and equip parents as the primary spiritual influencers of their children.

How will youth leaders do the most permanent good for the most teenagers? One hour in ministry to parents might affect more teenage lives than 10 hours of work directly with the teenagers. Changing a teenager's home is more likely to have a permanent impact on him or her than almost any other area of life.

The Bible says:

"We will not conceal [God's instruction] from their children, but tell to the generation to come the praises of the Lord, and His strength and His wondrous works that He has done.

"For He established a testimony in Jacob and appointed a law in Israel, which He commanded our fathers that they should teach them to their children, that the generation to come might know, even the children yet to be born, that they may arise and tell them to their children, that they should put their confidence in God and not forget the works of God, but keep His commandments" (Psalm 78:4-7).

Youth leaders equip parents to lead their children in informal ways. Informal spiritual impact:

- takes place as parents model truth and values in front of their children
- includes talks in the van on the way to soccer
- includes searching Scripture together when a child has a crisis
- includes the sparkle in parents' eyes as they tell children discoveries they are making about who Christ is today

11

Informal spiritual instruction in the home is vital but never can take the place of formal times the family gathers to talk about the things of God. Youth leaders may give parents a guide to know how best to plan family Bible study, how to pray together in a variety of ways, and how to make worship warm and relational.

Youth leaders equip parents to handle discipline biblically. Parents parent best when their parenting mirrors the way the Father parents them. He parents adults with a perfect balance of His justice and grace.

Modeling God's justice means parents are in authority over children. Parents make decisions about structure, limits, and behavior, and they enforce those decisions. Connecting bad behavior with negative consequences (discipline) is far more effective in changing the behavior than sharp words and anger. Parents also need to show children every time their good, biblical choices lead to positive, natural consequences.

Modeling God's grace means parents love teenagers without conditions. They communicate that there is nothing teenagers need to do, change, or accomplish to earn parents' love and acceptance. Parents show genuine interest and empathy in their lives.

Some church parents fearful of the world try to isolate their children from the lost. Those same parents probably hope their children will grow up to be strong adults who then will try to win the world to Jesus.

Unfortunately, a parent has no magic switch to throw that can change an older teenager's mind-set from "avoid lost people at all costs" to "redeem all persons to Christ." Parents who have reared the family with a bunker mentality probably will get young adults content to live out their lives in that bunker.

On the other hand, children who can't remember a time when family members weren't focused on lost friends and acquaintances will probably grow into young adults with a heart for the world. A heart for their "Jerusalem" will lead easily to a concern for the "uttermost parts of the earth" (see Acts 1:8).

Parents who are alive in Christ and who parent biblically will likely see their children, for the glory of the Father and in the power of the Spirit, spend a lifetime embracing the full supremacy of King Jesus.

TRUTH 6

Youth leaders guide teenagers to worship with awe intertwined with intimacy.

The primary purpose of human beings is to declare God's praise—"The people whom I formed for Myself will declare My praise" (Isaiah 43:21). God created teenagers, youth leaders, all humankind, and the universe for the display of His glory (Romans 1:20; Isaiah 43:6-7).

God calls His people to praise and glorify Him. Such worship is a human response to God's revelation. Teenagers and their leaders offer a spiritual response to God flowing out of their biblical understanding of God.

Worship can help move teenagers from being self-absorbed to being Christ-absorbed. Moses proclaimed, "Hear, O Israel! The Lord is our God, the Lord is one! You shall love the Lord your God with all your heart and with all your soul and with all your might" (Deuteronomy 6:4-5).

The goal of worship is not to feel better or be blessed. Worship is an action that involves the worshiper's whole being and should be directed toward God.

The work of Christ on the cross is the foundation of true worship. The Son of God came to the earth "to seek and to save that which was lost" (Luke 19:10) because "such people the Father seeks to be His worshipers" (John 4:23).

People primarily are redeemed to transform them into beings who can worship the Almighty. You and your teenagers now "have confidence to enter the holy place by the blood of Jesus, by a new and living way which He inaugurated for us through the veil, that is, His flesh" (Hebrews 10:19-20).

Paul taught that believers should "be filled with the Spirit, speaking to one another in psalms and hymns and spiritual songs, singing and making melody with your heart to the Lord" (Ephesians 5:18-19). The Spirit of God fills the hearts of His people with song.

Youth worship experiences must tread carefully in the area of teenage emotions. Youth leaders can manipulate the emotions of teenage worshipers.

Genuine worship certainly has an emotional element, but teenagers should be careful not to equate their own emotions with the person of the Holy Spirit. Youth leaders guide teenagers to test their experiences by the teaching of the Bible.

Leaders select worship music that guides teenagers to focus on lyrics rather than the music alone. The lyrics need to be biblically sound and should lead to Gospel-centered worship.

During youth group worship, youth leaders with cool hearts may chat with adult friends at the back of the room. Youth leaders with hearts overflowing with adoration toward the King join the teenagers as exuberant worshipers. Leaders influence teenagers in one of those two directions.

Youth group worship always is secondary to the worship of the full congregation. In both the Old and New Testaments, when God's people assembled for worship, all the generations typically were present (see Ezra 10:1; Nehemiah 8:1-2; Joel 2:15-16; and Acts 20:7-9). The segregation of age groups in worship is a more recent development.

Sunday morning worship is a multi-generational community of faith coming into the presence of God. Youth leaders equip teenagers to more fully participate in and appreciate corporate worship.

The openness of the youth group to the preaching of God's Word depends, in part, on their relationship to the pastor. Youth leaders who work to develop open and loving bonds between pastor and teenagers are laying the groundwork for worship.

Youth ministry exists to multiply worshipers of King Jesus, now and for eternity. Youth leaders who are genuine worshipers are the key.

TRUTH 7

Youth leaders share the Gospel with lost teenagers, and they lead others to do so.

Right before Jesus ascended, He told His disciples, "You shall be My witnesses" (Acts 1:8). Witnessing is simply sharing the Gospel with those separated from Christ. Although not all youth leaders can share the Gospel to the remotest parts of the earth, they can witness to the teenagers in their areas of influence.

While on earth, Jesus often spoke of a literal hell. According to Scripture, all who die without accepting God's gift of salvation through Jesus Christ will continue to be separated from God in hell for eternity—"He who believes in the Son has eternal life; but he who does not obey the Son will not see life, but the wrath of God abides on him" (John 3:36).

What do teenagers have to do to go to hell? The answer is nothing. Teenagers are born separated from God (Psalm 51:5). When infants and very young children die, they go to heaven only because a special grace from God covers them. But when children reach an age at which they can understand the Gospel, that special grace no longer is available.

At that time, they stand in danger of hell—not because of a particular sin, but because they always have been separated from God. Unless a miracle takes place, they will be separated from God in torment forever.

Teenagers are searching for what Christ has to offer. Their lives often are characterized by inner emptiness, purposelessness, fear of death, desire for inner peace, loneliness, and lack of self-control. Such teenagers are "distressed and dispirited like sheep without a shepherd" (Matthew 9:36). They need Jesus.

Lost teenagers also need to be redeemed because of the potential they represent for the Kingdom. Every life is full of potential to glorify God, but teenagers can only fulfill that potential in a relationship with Christ.

Youth leaders present the Gospel to the lost, in part, for their own spiritual well-being. Sharing Jesus naturally leads to adoring Him more.

> It's like what often is observed when a bride-to-be eagerly reports to all her girlfriends what a wonderful man her future husband is to her. To her amazement, the very act of sharing him with others ends up deepening her own longings and passions for him as well.[4]

Also, nothing refreshes the soul like the fresh joy of a teenager's meeting Jesus. Witnessing a new birth from time to time can make up for some hard days in ministry.

Everything done in youth ministry should have as its ultimate goal the winning of lost teenagers to Jesus Christ.

- Discipleship should strengthen believing teenagers for the task of sharing the Gospel.
- Worship should prepare the hearts of teenagers for sharing their faith.
- Social events should build relationships so that teenagers and their leaders can share the Good News.

Reaching out must be a priority. The youth budget should reflect it. The agendas of gatherings should reflect it. The youth calendar should reflect it. Youth leaders who adore King Jesus join Him in accelerating the harvest. David Bryant concludes:

> Here's one crucial way fervency for Jesus' supremacy expresses itself: by our determination to *share* him and his gospel with those who are lost, doing so in such a way that we exalt his name to them, spread his fame around them, extend his reign among them, increase his gain from them, and ratify his claim before them.[5]

TRUTH 8

Youth leaders guide teenagers to so love Jesus that they introduce others to Him locally and globally.

Our King's command is crystal clear:

"All authority has been given to Me in heaven and on earth. Go therefore and make disciples of all the nations, baptizing them in the name of the Father and the Son and the Holy Spirit, teaching them to observe all that I commanded you; and lo, I am with you always, even to the end of the age" (Matthew 28:18–20).

Youth leaders who love and obey Jesus evangelize teenagers, transform converts into disciples, and mobilize disciples to evangelize locally and globally—all in the power of the Spirit.

Jesus is our model, not merely as a guide but as the personification of discipleship. He not only called and led the disciples and others to Himself, but loved them, taught them, trained them, equipped them, and sent them out to do as He had done (Matthew 28:19; Mark 11:17; 16:15-16).[6]

Youth ministry is not a place where the next generation is told to sit down and be quiet. Instead, teenagers are called to stand up and step out. Boldness takes the place of timidity (see Acts 28:31; Ephesians 6:19). Teenagers do not find this boldness deep within themselves. They discover boldness by depending on the power and presence of Jesus Christ and the Holy Spirit who indwells all believers (see Matthew 28:18-20; Acts 1:8).

Twelve-year-olds are fully capable of sharing the Gospel locally and regionally. (In fact, grade-schoolers are as well.) Parents and youth leaders link arms to see young youth group members approach their middle school as a mission field.

Fifteen-year-olds are fully capable of sharing the Gospel across the nation. Because of its size and spiritual lethargy, the U.S. now has one of the larger populations of lost persons.

Eighteen-year-olds are fully capable of leveraging their lives for the sake of the Gospel internationally. During high school, that may mean two weeks in a distant land. After high school graduation, that may mean a summer, semester, or a year. After college graduation, that may mean a couple of years planting the church domestically or globally.

Youth ministries that do not preach and teach about missions, do not pray for missions, do not raise funds for missions, and do not take teenagers to be part of missions:

1. *Can lead to teenagers who do not hear a short-term or lifetime call to global or domestic missions.*
   Certainly, youth ministry experiences do not "call" them into missions, but those experiences create an environment where teenagers can be sensitive to God's calling.

2. *Can lead to anemic prayer and giving toward global and domestic missions.*
   Teenagers who graduate from the youth group without a heart for this nation and the world will become church members and leaders without a heart for missions.

3. *Can lead to incomplete transformation.*
   Worship, Bible study, and discipleship are receiving ministries. Missions is a giving ministry. Receiving without giving leads to spiritual stagnation.

Youth ministry develops teenagers who so love Jesus that they introduce others to Him locally and globally, now and for a lifetime.

TRUTH 9

Youth leaders guide teenagers to love others more than they love themselves.

If you are a believer, then "you shall love the Lord your God with all your heart and with all your soul and with all your might" (Deuteronomy 6:5). Jesus called this the "Great Commandment" (see Matthew 22:36–38). Youth leaders embrace this call and seek to lead Great Commandment ministries.

The second greatest commandment is to "love your neighbor as yourself" (Matthew 22:39). "For all eternity, love has reigned supreme. Before anything was made—before there were any humans to forgive or restore or reconcile or embrace—still love existed."[7] Such love defines the core of God's nature—"God is love" (1 John 4:8).

Jesus said, "By this all men will know that you are My disciples, if you have love for one another" (John 13:35). The Christian community is to "be identified by the quality of one member's love for another."[8] Love, then, is the mark of a true disciple, and love should be the mark of any healthy youth ministry. Such love allows a Great Commandment youth ministry to flourish in the local church and lovingly impact the community with the Gospel.

A loving ministry is one that meets another person's need in the name of Jesus. Ministry grows out of a transformed and serving life. Ministry is the normal function of every believer.

Teenage disciples who follow Jesus will share His heart for those in need.

It's clear that the Bible instructs God's people to serve the poor. If we want students to practice a biblical faith, youth leaders must train and equip them to serve the poor in a way that is helpful and honors God. This is a matter, simply, of obedience to God's Word![9]

Teenage believers express loving compassion toward the total person: "Get [your teenagers] to feed the poor with bread AND the Bread of Life. Have them pass out water for the body AND Living Water for the soul. Get your teenagers to build houses for the poor on earth AND ones in heaven too."[10]

Meeting someone's practical need only as a sneaky way to present the Gospel is not the compassion of Christ. On the other hand, only meeting practical needs and never sharing the Good News also is disobedient to Scripture. Teenage disciples sacrificially care for others. And they always direct attention to Jesus as the Spirit leads.

Read Matthew 25:37-40 slowly and carefully:

> "Then the righteous will answer Him, 'Lord, when did we see You hungry, and feed You, or thirsty, and give You something to drink? And when did we see You a stranger, and invite You in, or naked, and clothe You? When did we see You sick, or in prison, and come to You?'
>
> "The King will answer and say to them, 'Truly I say to you, to the extent that you did it to one of these brothers of Mine, even the least of them, you did it to Me.'"

"Jesus is saying that we show tangible love for God in how we care for the poor and those who are suffering. He expects us to treat the poor and the desperate as if they were Christ Himself."[11]

Fear and guilt are not proper motivation for sacrificial love. God's Son wants teenagers to love others extravagantly because those teenagers are overwhelmingly in love with Him. Galatians 5:13-14 says:

> "For you were called to freedom, brethren; only do not turn your freedom into an opportunity for the flesh, but through love serve one another. For the whole Law is fulfilled in one word, in the statement, 'You shall love your neighbor as yourself.'"

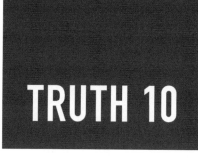

TRUTH 10

Youth leaders guide teenagers to know that their identity is in Christ.

Even some teenagers at church might say: "I'm of little value since my body does not match the stereotypes of society." "I'm of little value since the timetable for my sexual development is different from others." "I'm of little value since I cannot yet identify my gifts, strengths, and abilities." "I'm just the product of random chance at the time of my conception."

The teenage years are an important time in establishing identity. Scars that last a lifetime can occur as teenagers come to negative conclusions about their bodies, abilities, and related issues. Humanistic explanations about their worth and value are hollow.

But what if teenagers are surrounded with people who are becoming more and more alive to the Lord Jesus Christ? What if they peer into the DNA of youth leaders with whom they share life and they can see identities grounded in Christ? Who those adults are will simply amplify and confirm what they teach from Scripture about true identity. The Word of God and the people of God have much to offer during this process.

Building a worldview is part of solidifying an identity. Teenagers form a worldview by answering ultimate questions, such as: What is real? What is true? What is beautiful? What is of value? Why am I here? What does all this mean?

Teenagers want and need a worldview that gives a consistent and all-encompassing perspective on life and the universe. Young believers who absorb Scripture find the only accurate view of existence and thus the only real foundation for an identity.

Young disciples can embrace the fact that each of them is a special creation, designed by God Himself—"You formed my inward parts; You wove me in my mother's womb. I will give thanks to You, for I am fearfully and wonderfully made; wonderful are Your works, and my soul knows it very well" (Psalm 139:13-14).

Teenagers establish identities in part through relationships. Through experiences in groups, teenagers learn more about themselves, including strengths and weaknesses.

Not all groups are equal in their contributions to healthy identities. Groups at church can have a decided advantage over many of the groups available to teenagers. Groups that reflect the spirit of Christ can be honest, accepting, and supportive of teenagers solidifying an identity.

Teenagers also form identities through relationships with significant adults. Most teenagers create a bit of distance between themselves and their parents during middle and high school. During this time, teenagers are open to relationships with other significant adults. Youth leaders who exude Jesus can see their DNA being transferred to young disciples. Outside the church, teenagers find a severe shortage of adults who care about them and who are solid role models.

Teenagers solidifying identities also need a clear picture of the ideal person they are seeking to become. The church offers teenagers the only genuine ideal—Jesus Christ. Young disciples need to see their "Royal Redeemer for who he really is: high and lifted up; seated at the helm of the universe; ruling triumphantly at this very moment from the center of God's throne; Head of the Church; Lord and Master of all who trust in him."[12]

Any ideal other than Jesus is second-rate. Paul wrote, "Therefore if anyone is in Christ, he is a new creature; the old things passed away; behold, new things have come" (2 Corinthians 5:17).

King Jesus is the true picture of man's highest being. Scripture calls all believers to be conformed to His image (Romans 8:29). He is the center of any true identity.

Forever, his story has become our story;
his identity, our identity;
and his destiny our destiny.[13]

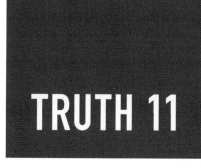

TRUTH 11

Youth leaders guide teenagers to find in Christ their all-consuming purpose.

A family, youth ministry, and church exist for the glory of God. In the same way, a teenage believer exists for the glory of God. Scripture could not be clearer (emphasis added):

> "Therefore, having been justified by faith, we have peace with God through our Lord Jesus Christ, through whom also we have obtained our introduction by faith into this grace in which we stand; and we exult in hope of *the glory of God*" (Romans 5:1-2).

> "Whether, then, you eat or drink or whatever you do, do all to *the glory of God*" (1 Corinthians 10:31).

The true goal of youth ministry is to see teenagers who have hearts filled with hot magma—that rushes to the surface and bursts out in worship, holiness, and Kingdom acts—for *the glory of God*. That magma is Word-formed and Spirit-enabled awe and intimacy with King Jesus.

Youth leaders continually ask: "Are we consistently introducing teenagers to Jesus and then discipling them into believers who will, for a lifetime, love God, love people, and make disciples for *the glory of God*?"

Youth ministry develops teenagers who risk everything to be abandoned to Jesus and to make the Gospel known among all peoples. They have faces set like flint to fulfill their purpose on the earth. Increasingly, they can join Paul in saying:

> "But whatever things were gain to me, those things I have counted as loss for the sake of Christ. More than that, I count all things to be loss in view of the surpassing value of

knowing Christ Jesus my Lord, for whom I have suffered the loss of all things, and count them but rubbish so that I may gain Christ" (Philippians 3:7-8).

What do young disciples count as loss? Here are just a few items:

1. *Possessions.*

Jesus said to a young man, "One thing you lack: go and sell all you possess and give to the poor, and you will have treasure in heaven; and come, follow Me" (Mark 10:21). Jesus may or may not ask you or your teenagers to sell everything. But He calls you to be willing to do so.

2. *Fame.*

For a season, John the Baptist was a rock star. Both rich and poor filled large crowds hanging on his every word. But when it was time for the Messiah's public ministry to begin, John was quick to shift the spotlight to Him. John said, "He must increase, but I must decrease" (John 3:30).

3. *Relationships.*

Believers must ask themselves: "If some extreme situation required that I make a choice, would I count *every* human relationship as loss—for His surpassing greatness?" (see Luke 14:26).

4. *One's Physical Life.*

School shootings and terrorism are becoming common. Teenagers in the U.S. now join young believers worldwide in having to decide: "Will I, at this moment, lay down my life to be true to my beloved Savior?"

A powerful way to see teenagers find their all-encompassing purpose in Christ is to give them heart connections with youth leaders who find their all-encompassing purpose in Christ. Would that be you?

TRUTH 12

Youth leaders guide teenagers to serve joyfully out of gratitude for the Gospel and Christ's completed work.

Many teenagers who know that grace redeemed them seem to believe that same grace is not sufficient for growing in Christ. They approach service and discipleship as duties. They quietly believe that only through their efforts can they stay in God's favor and accomplish anything worthwhile. For them, following the Way is mostly a drudgery.

But here is the paradox. Those who only grit their teeth and try harder don't grow much. On the other hand...

> Those people who get better are those who understand that God's approval of them is not dependent on their getting better. ... Abiding in Jesus will produce all of the fruits of the Spirit in you—but not by having you concentrate particularly on any of those things. You concentrate on Jesus. You rest in His love and acceptance, given to you not because of what you have earned, but because of what He has earned for you.[14]

Far too many teenage believers try to work up enough willpower to obey instead of trusting in Christ's finished work and the Spirit's power. They need some good news:

> It's never a question of whether we are to obey God. ... But whenever we teach the Scriptures, it is crucial to stress this point: God doesn't begin with commands. He begins by demonstrating what He has done for His people. ... That takes away our need to earn God's favor because He lavishly pours

it out upon us through Jesus. ... This is the good news God gives us.[15]

Teenage believers need a full-bodied understanding of the Gospel—the incarnation, crucifixion, resurrection, and ascension of the Messiah.

The gospel is that Christ has suffered the full wrath of God for my sin. ... He actually became my sin so that I could literally become His righteousness. ... When I receive that grace in repentance and faith, full acceptance becomes mine. ... That means that God could not love me any more than He does right now, because God could not love and accept Christ any more than He does, and God sees me in Christ.[16]

True believers find in the cross the source of their salvation *and* grace for living, serving, and growing.

The majesty of the perfect One who descended from heaven to die for us undercuts every conceivable pretext about our ability to reconcile with God by our own moral achievements. For if there were any other way to secure eternal life for us, then clearly Christ's agonies were horribly wasted and utterly tragic.[17]

What about you? Would your teenagers say you abide in Christ and joyfully live and serve out of grace and gratitude? Are you joyfully saturated with the incarnation, crucifixion, resurrection, and ascension of Jesus? If so, then join the Father in saying to Jesus:

All you have accomplished for my people by your incarnation,
your life of righteousness, your teachings and healings,
your atoning sacrifice, and your definitive disabling of
death are *totally sufficient*! You have fulfilled all that's needed
for the reclamation of the universe.
So come, my Son, take the crown and the glory; begin to reign as
King of kings and Lord of lords, forever and ever![18]

TRUTH 13

Youth leaders draw every element of their youth ministries from the Bible.

Youth leaders are wise to draw every element of their youth ministry from the pages of God's Word. This is true for several reasons.

Scripture is the living and active Word of God (Hebrews 4:12). Scripture is God's revelation of Himself to man (Romans 1:17). Scripture is inspired by God (2 Timothy 3:16) and is without error from beginning to end. Scripture is the sole authority for life and godly living (2 Peter 1:3).

God alone knows what ministry design will accomplish His eternal purposes—"Many plans are in a man's heart, but the counsel of the Lord will stand" (Proverbs 19:21). Even Jesus said, "Whatever the Father does, these things the Son also does in like manner. For the Father loves the Son, and shows Him all things that He Himself is doing" (John 5:19-20).

Youth leaders are sent by King Jesus to establish His Kingdom in the lives of teenagers and their families. One by one, as leaders redeem them, equip them, disciple them, and send them, leaders establish His Kingdom. Youth leaders find their ways of doing just that in the pages of God's Word.

Why do youth leaders do what they do? Why do they take valuable time from their own families to do youth ministry? Why do they sometimes work to exhaustion? Why do they spend Kingdom money? The answer should be that the youth leaders have drawn what they are doing from the pages of Scripture and thus are moving with God's brilliance.

Scores of passages should establish all that leaders do in youth ministry. The following Scriptures will certainly be on that list:

1. Declaring God's Praise:
"The people whom I formed for Myself will declare My praise" (Isaiah 43:21).

2. The Reign of Christ:
"God highly exalted Him, and bestowed on Him the name which is above every name, so that at the name of Jesus every knee will bow, of those who are in heaven and on earth and under the earth, and that every tongue will confess that Jesus Christ is Lord, to the glory of God the Father" (Philippians 2:9-11).

3. The Great Commission:
"All authority has been given to Me in heaven and on earth. Go therefore and make disciples of all the nations, baptizing them in the name of the Father and the Son and the Holy Spirit, teaching them to observe all that I commanded you; and lo, I am with you always, even to the end of the age" (Matthew 28:18-20).

4. The Great Commandment:
"And [Jesus] said to him, 'You shall love the Lord your God with all your heart, and with all your soul, and with all your mind.' This is the great and foremost commandment. The second is like it, 'You shall love your neighbor as yourself'" (Matthew 22:37–39).

5. Congregational Life:
"So then, those who had received his word were baptized. … They were continually devoting themselves to the apostles' teaching and to fellowship, to the breaking of bread and to prayer" (Acts 2:41-42).

6. Servanthood:
"Whoever wishes to be first among you shall be slave of all. For even the Son of Man did not come to be served, but to serve, and to give His life a ransom for many" (Mark 10:44-45).

King Jesus stands ready to reveal His plans to you,
using His Word, illuminated by His Spirit,
for the glory of His Father.

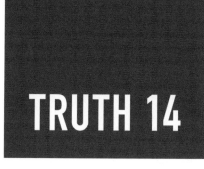

TRUTH 14

Youth leaders plan youth ministry worthy of the King.

Youth ministry is purposeful and consistently moves toward a goal. One way to express the end goal of youth ministry is this:

Students who, for the glory of the Father and in the power of the Spirit, spend a lifetime embracing the full supremacy of the Son, responding to His majesty in all of life, inviting Christ to live His life through them, and joining Him in making disciples among all peoples.

One factor that determines whether youth ministry achieves its goals is planning. Solomon wrote, "The plans of the diligent lead surely to advantage, but everyone who is hasty comes surely to poverty" (Proverbs 21:5).

Planning has a role in a prosperous, growing, and Kingdom-advancing youth ministry. Leaders with a youth group of two plan with the same excellence as leaders with a youth group of a thousand. Nehemiah faced the task of rebuilding the walls of Jerusalem. Nehemiah moved forward with confidence because he took time to plan. The book of Nehemiah provides several habits for effective planning.

The first habit of effective planning is praying. Nehemiah discovered that the remnant who survived exile were in distress, and enemies had destroyed the walls of Jerusalem. The first thing Nehemiah did when he heard the troubling news was pray (Nehemiah 1:4). The task of youth ministry is beyond human strength, so wise leaders saturate that ministry with prayer. God reveals His plans when His people call on Him.

The second habit of effective planning is developing a strategy. Nehemiah knew how long the project would take (Nehemiah 2:6). He knew he would need safe passage to Jerusalem and what supplies he would need (Nehemiah 2:7-8). Nehemiah had a plan, and youth leaders today need one too.

The third habit of effective planning is leading the way. Nehemiah did not try to build a wall alone. Instead, he led the nation of Israel to build the wall. The Jewish remnant moved forward with courage because of Nehemiah's inspirational leadership. Teenagers will follow credible and passionate leaders who know where they are going.

Planning is vital in Kingdom-advancing youth ministries. Kingdom advancement happens when youth leaders humble themselves in prayer, create a plan, and confidently lead with credibility, passion, and direction.

Careful planning makes it more likely that leaders take steps on time. Timely planned steps usually take half as long and are twice as effective as steps taken at the last minute.

Careful planning permits the youth calendar to mesh with the full church program. The era when youth ministry was a world unto itself is over.

Careful planning allows families to plan their lives. Parents are not as likely to get behind spur-of-the-moment plans.

Careful planning provides time to involve more people. The advantages of involving more people in youth ministry are obvious. Working alone usually happens as a result of not doing proper planning.

The criteria for evaluating youth ministry is this question: Are we consistently introducing teenagers to King Jesus and then discipling them into believers who will, for *a lifetime*, love God, love people, and make disciples for the glory of God? Youth leaders and core teenagers, with Bibles open and eyes lifted in prayer, can find God's unique plan for moving them in those directions. Here is their motivation:

Clearly, Christians can never think too highly of God's Son
or put too much passion into advancing his kingdom agenda.
An all-consuming devotion, an overt obsession, a fanatical focus,
a supreme fervency—it all denotes the chief hallmark
of every Jesus follower, in which there can be no turning back
and no holding back from him.[19]

TRUTH 15

Youth leaders make disciples who make disciples for a lifetime.

For the glory of God, in the power of the Spirit, youth leaders make disciples who make disciples among all peoples. Jesus does not charge the church to make converts but to make disciples.

After God raised Jesus from the dead, the disciples went to the mountain Jesus designated in Galilee. Jesus gave them the Great Commission:

> "And Jesus came up and spoke to them, saying, 'All authority has been given to Me in heaven and on earth. Go therefore and make disciples of all the nations, baptizing them in the name of the Father and the Son and the Holy Spirit, teaching them to observe all that I commanded you; and lo, I am with you always, even to the end of the age'" (Matthew 28:18–20).

Youth leaders need to understand terms regarding discipleship:

- "Clearly, back in the first century when the New Testament was written, the word [*disciple*] was used to refer to adherents or followers of a great master—not just a teacher-student relationship, but a master-follower relationship."[20]
- The word *discipleship* refers to "a lifelong journey of obedience to Christ which transforms a person's values and behavior, and results in ministry to one's home, church, and in the world."[21]
- *Disciplemaking* is "intentionally equipping believers with the Word of God through accountable relationships empowered by the Holy Spirit in order to replicate faithful followers of Christ."[22]

God has a plan for bringing His Kingdom on earth. "From the start, God's simple design has been for every single disciple of Jesus to make disciples who make disciples who make disciples until the gospel spreads to all people in the planet."[23]

As quickly as possible, a teenager needs to learn to take the initiative for his or her spiritual growth. Today, many adults in the church never have begun to do that. Youth leaders cannot be content to produce even more adults in that condition. Beyond taking responsibility for their spiritual growth, teenage disciples need to prepare to disciple someone else.

A discipleship process must not lead to teenagers who just sit and listen. The goal of discipleship is not only making disciples. The goal is making disciples so enthralled with Jesus, so full of His aroma, and so expressive of His life that *they* make disciples. They become high school graduates who are motivated and equipped to disciple others in college, trade school, the military, the workplace, or the home.

"The Master who marched out of a graveyard to ascend to the throne of the universe deserves radical commitment from teenagers and leaders—as He spelled it out in Scriptures."[24]

- "If anyone wishes to come after Me, he must deny himself, and take up his cross and follow Me. For whoever wishes to save his life will lose it, but whoever loses his life for My sake and the gospel's will save it" (Mark 8:34–35).
- "He who loves father or mother more than Me is not worthy of Me; and he who loves son or daughter more than Me is not worthy of Me. … He who has found his life will lose it, and he who has lost his life for My sake will find it" (Matthew 10:37, 39).

Fervency for the supremacy of the Savior requires every born-again heart to be increasingly wrapped up in the totality of who Christ is right now. No turning back. No holding back. Not now. Not ever.[25]

TRUTH 16

Youth leaders unleash God's Word in the hearts and minds of teenagers.

The Bible is sufficient to guide Christ-followers. Youth leaders should see God's Word consistently unleashed in the hearts and minds of teenagers.

God wants to transform teenagers' hearts with His Word—"For the word of God is living and active and sharper than any two-edged sword, and piercing as far as the division of soul and spirit, of both joints and marrow, and able to judge the thoughts and intentions of the heart" (Hebrews 4:12).

Paul knew the value of God's Word. In his ministry with young Timothy, Paul encouraged him to continue to learn from the Scriptures. Paul knew that God's Word was sufficient and that it could reach into every area of Timothy's life.

Here is what Paul said about the sufficiency of Scripture: "All Scripture is inspired by God and profitable for *teaching*, for *reproof*, for *correction*, for *training* in righteousness; so that the man of God may be adequate, equipped for every good work" (2 Timothy 3:16-17, emphasis added). Youth leaders follow these same four steps.

1. *First, youth leaders let the Scripture teach.* God has given Christ-followers everything they need for life and godly living. The Scripture equips teenagers by teaching them. Young believers need God's Word more than man's observations.

2. *Second, youth leaders let the Scripture rebuke*, or admonish. The Word of God cuts deep to the joints and marrow, challenging teenagers with their need for change or adjustment. Rebuke reveals sin, confronts disobedience, and equips teenagers with tools to make course adjustments.

3. *Third, youth leaders let the Scripture correct.* "As Scripture rebukes us, it reveals our sin and shows us how to and why we should change. Our next step is correcting our course, changing our path, and developing new habits."[26] The Scripture equips teenagers by giving correction.
4. *Finally, youth leaders let the Scripture train.* "Training in righteousness is the counterpoint to correction. The Scriptures give us positive guidance for maturing in faith and acceptable conduct."[27] Rebuking reveals what is wrong. Correcting reveals the way to get right. Training helps the individual to stay right. The Scripture equips teenagers by training them to live godly lives consistently.

For decades, the goal of some youth classes has been to lead teenagers to understand and then apply the Bible. Understanding and application are part of the process, but some leaders might skip the step that must come in between.

Change in a believer's heart precedes outward change—"The good man out of the good treasure of his heart brings forth what is good; and the evil man out of the evil treasure brings forth what is evil; for his mouth speaks from that which fills his heart" (Luke 6:45).

Bible study that always makes a beeline to the glory and kingship of Jesus leads to heart transformation that then leads to application and changed behavior. Therefore, the flow of Bible study becomes (1) motivation, (2) examination, (3) adoration, and *then* (4) application.

To say this another way, "Repentance isn't just about what we turn from; it is also about what we turn toward, or rather Who we turn toward—the Christ who goes before us."[28] As stated in Hebrews 12:1-2,

> "Let us also lay aside every encumbrance and the sin which so easily entangles us, and let us run with endurance the race that is set before us, fixing our eyes on Jesus, the author and perfecter of faith, who for the joy set before Him endured the cross, despising the shame, and has sat down at the right hand of the throne of God."

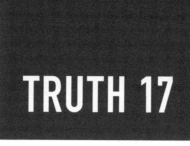

TRUTH 17

Youth leaders equip teenagers to articulate, defend, and live out the faith that is in them.

Picture a generation of teenagers who love Christ with all their heart, soul, mind, and strength. Picture teenagers who adore the King and would lay down their lives for Him. Picture teenagers who therefore are not bound to the culture. A generation such as that can change the world.

For teenage Christ-followers, the beginning point is what they believe. A leader might say, "When I hear what some of our church teenagers have been doing, I'm so frustrated. Why can't they live consistently with their beliefs?"

In reality, those teenagers *are* living consistently with their beliefs—their true beliefs—and not necessarily with their professed beliefs. How people behave reveals what they truly believe. *Being* always precedes *doing*.

When you are teaching teenagers, how can you tell if they are forming biblically sound beliefs in their minds and hearts? Ask them to say in their own words what they have come to believe. Then compare their answers to the clear teaching of Scripture.

Asking questions about beliefs may be rare at church. As part of the largest study of church teenagers, researchers conducted face-to-face interviews with thousands. The interviewers were uniformly amazed at how poorly most church teenagers did trying to express their beliefs.

The researchers concluded, "Indeed, it was our distinct sense that for many of the teens we interviewed, our interview was the first time that any adult had ever asked them what they believed and how it mattered in their lives."[29] Teenagers who only listen do not learn to articulate what they believe.

If Peter were alive today, he would probably challenge teenagers to "sanctify Christ as Lord in your hearts, always being ready to make a defense to everyone who asks you to give an account for the hope that is in you, yet with gentleness and reverence" (1 Peter 3:15).

Leaders who teach, listen to feedback, and then make adjustments will find teenagers able to say,

> "We are no longer to be children, tossed here and there by waves and carried about by every wind of doctrine, by the trickery of men, by craftiness in deceitful scheming; but speaking the truth in love, we are to grow up in all aspects into Him who is the head, even Christ" (Ephesians 4:14-15).

Teenagers today live in a secular world, daily navigating a culture that knows nothing of Christ, His values, or His Word. The current of the cultural streams proves strong, often pulling teenagers further and further away from God's truth. Youth leaders equip this generation to engage the non-Christian culture around them biblically.

When Jesus spoke about the pull to conform to the culture, He taught His followers that their identity is found in Him and not in the world. Jesus offered three different pictures in the Sermon on the Mount to lead His young disciples to engage the culture around them. He called them the salt of the earth, the light of the world, and a city on a hill (Matthew 5:13-14).

Teenagers need to know how to humbly, gently, but boldly apply the principles of Scripture to life while navigating a pluralistic culture. Why? For the glory of the King!

> "[God] raised Him from the dead and seated Him
> at His right hand in the heavenly places, far above all rule
> and authority and power and dominion, and every name that is
> named, not only in this age but also in the one to come"
> (Ephesians 1:20-21).

TRUTH 18

Youth leaders guide teenagers to embrace the spiritual disciplines.

The greatest need youth leaders and teenagers have is the renovation of their hearts. And what is the heart? "That spiritual place within us from which outlook, choices, and actions come has been formed by a world away from God. Now it must be transformed."[30]

One name for this process of transformation is spiritual formation. Spiritual formation refers to "the Spirit-driven process of forming the inner world of the human self in such a way that it becomes like the inner being of Christ himself."[31] When inner transformation happens, the outer life of a leader or teenager becomes "a natural expression or outflow of the character and teachings of Jesus."[32]

The Christian life begins with redemption by Jesus. Salvation leads to the transformation of the heart in the direction of the inner being of Jesus. Such an inner transformation leads naturally to outer obedience or conformity to Jesus. From beginning to end, Jesus is the focus.

Believers who hunger to be like Jesus cooperate with the Spirit of God as He transforms their hearts. Among the tools the Spirit uses are, first and foremost, the Word of God and, second, the influence of those in whom Christ is most alive.

Youth leaders have the amazing privilege of teaching teenagers those Scripture passages that the Spirit will use to transform hearts. Heart change always is the immediate goal in Bible teaching. Only inner transformation will lead to obedience and conformity to Jesus for a lifetime.

Youth leaders also have the privilege of allowing teenagers to peer into the leader's heart. The Spirit uses the transformation of more mature believers to inspire and instruct newer believers in the same directions.

Leaders who are transparent and open see more change in teenagers than those who are reserved and hide behind "the lesson." Leaders who share life with teenagers away from church see more change than those who only connect in classrooms.

Neither leaders nor teenagers can sit back and wait for transformation to happen. "While [transformation] is simultaneously a profound manifestation of God's gracious action through his Word and Spirit, it is also something we are responsible for before God and can set about achieving in a sensible, systemic manner."[33]

The sensible and systematic steps the believer can take are the spiritual disciplines. Youth leaders possess an incredible opportunity to bless teenagers for a lifetime as they prompt the practice of spiritual disciplines.

Among the disciplines are:

- Memorizing Scripture
- Solitude (being alone with God for long periods of time)
- Fasting (learning freedom from food and how God directly nourishes us)
- Worship (adoration of God)
- Service (doing good for others with no thought of ourselves)

Prayer is one of the most important spiritual disciplines. Jesus prayed. He prayed in power, He prayed for others, He prayed for Himself, He prayed in need, and He prayed in celebration. Jesus modeled prayer, taught prayer, encouraged prayer, corrected wrongness of prayer, and held His followers accountable in the practice of prayer.

What if teenagers came to your home for your early morning prayers? What if you prayed out loud for their benefit? Would they hear in your voice your intimate adoration of Christ enthroned? Would they hear brokenness as you confess sin? Would they hear you joyfully express thanks for Christ's blessings? Would they hear you intercede for Kingdom concerns before you make requests for yourself?

Here is an exciting thought. As the Spirit increasingly transforms your heart and you go to new places in prayer, you can take teenagers with you. And for many of them, those journeys will last a lifetime.

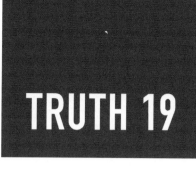

TRUTH 19

Youth leaders welcome teenagers' honest doubts and questions.

Some youth leaders might assume that doubt is an issue for only a handful of teenagers. They would be surprised to discover that the vast majority of church teenagers have such thoughts.[34] Sadly, one in 10 of those teenagers would agree with the statement, "I am not allowed to talk about my doubts in church."[35]

Even the stalwart John the Baptist sought an attitudinal realignment from Jesus when facing doubts (Matthew 11:1-6). John was in prison, and though originally confident in Christ, he later faced some doubts. That prompted John to send messengers to Jesus.

Today, the culture strongly challenges teenagers to abandon their faith. At the very least, they are challenged to acknowledge that their faith is just one of many equally true and useful religious perspectives. They also are challenged to doubt whether absolute truth or moral authority exists in the universe.

God is not offended by honest questions. In fact, He welcomes them. Youth leaders and parents should follow His example. They need to rest in the confidence that the Christian faith as presented in Scripture is not going to collapse because one of their teenagers thought of a question.

Leaders show confidence that they believe the Christian faith is rock-solid. But at the same time, they can humbly confess that they do not have every answer on the tip of their tongues. "When we honestly don't know what to say at the time, we will just say so. We will go away and find an answer through study, conversation, and prayer."[36]

Wise and experienced youth leaders tend to say:

> We then listen prayerfully to those we teach. We encourage every question, and we make it clear that dealing honestly with the questions that come up is the only path to a robust

and healthy faith. We never "pooh-pooh" difficulties, or take any problem with anything less than utter seriousness, or direct the slightest reproach or shame on anyone for having questions and doubts.[37]

Sometimes teenagers experience doubt after experiencing a moral failure. They may feel so guilty that they begin to doubt their faith. "When you're engaged in behavior you've been raised to believe is wrong, but is still pretty fun, more than that, powerfully enslaving, you want to find reasons to disbelieve your former moral convictions."[38]

Teenagers need to transfer the doctrine of God's absolute forgiveness from their heads to their hearts. Those with doubt flowing from guilt are just as likely as other teenagers to affirm that God forgives them.

Though intellectually they acknowledge God's forgiveness, emotionally they do not live in an awareness of God's acceptance. The antidote is a more complete understanding of grace and the Gospel.

Neither intellectual doubt nor doubt flowing from guilt is necessarily destructive. The key is how parents and leaders respond. Those who study teenagers closely can conclude: "Most church teenagers doubt their faith. For a variety of reasons, few of them talk about those doubts. But those who feel most free to express doubts and discuss personal problems with youth leaders and peers show more lifetime faith."[39]

Youth leaders and parents can create an atmosphere that permits teenagers to express their doubts. They can walk beside teenagers as they press toward answers together. If they do, they will see many more young adults declare to Christ:

Ascended, anointed, and crowned as supreme in all things,
today you are filling the universe with your sovereignty,
your majesty, your activity, and your presence.
Come, therefore; set up your throne among us,
right here and right now.[40]

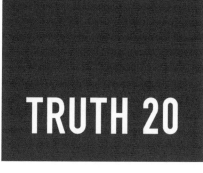

TRUTH 20

Youth leaders love and relate to teenagers the way Jesus does.

Christ absolutely adores His Father and enjoys a deep relationship with Him. The same is true about every relationship in the Godhead. Jesus wants all believers to know such rich relationships.

The King desires that "they may all be one; even as You, Father, are in Me and I in You, that they also may be in Us, so that the world may believe that You sent Me" (John 17:21).

Leaders love every teenager because every teenager is a unique creation of God. Incredible as it may seem to some, every teenager carries the image of God.

Wise youth leaders love teenagers as they use words of affirmation. The "vocabulary of affirmation" contains expressions such as:

- "The church isn't the same when you are gone."
- "Those who know you best have confidence in your future."
- "Knowing you has made me a better person."
- "I know God has special plans for you."
- "We love watching God reveal the gifts and abilities He has placed inside you."

Some youth leaders minister most to the teenagers who need it least. Jesus did the opposite. Daily, He gave time to those with the greatest needs. Lepers and prostitutes might not be welcome in some churches, but they were important to Jesus.

Godly youth leaders avoid a marketplace mentality that communicates, "I will give you my attention and approval in exchange for your contribution to the success of my program." Hurting teenagers have gifts to use in the work of the Kingdom, but their gifts may be buried deeply. Those teenagers need a personal touch of ministry even if it is a long time before they can discover and use those gifts.

Some leaders want a youth group that looks good to the congregation. Such leaders may wonder if their reputations will suffer if "freaky-looking" teenagers start showing up.

When Jesus had to choose between His reputation with superficial adults and meeting genuine needs, He always went with meeting needs. Adults who love Jesus will appreciate a ministry to those who need it most.

Ministry to those who need it most is hard work. Usually, those teenagers come from homes with more problems that need more ministry. Needy teenagers may be more undisciplined or starved for individual attention. They get in more messes that take time to straighten out.

Youth leaders need a heart like the heart of Jesus to minister to the teenagers who need it most. Zacchaeus went up the tree a desperate man, and he came down changed by the love of Jesus. An openness to such a ministry marks a step toward spiritual maturity in the life of the leader.

Needy teenagers usually have a hard time expressing love and gratitude. They may not give leaders as many positive strokes as better-adjusted teens. Marketplace love says, "I will love you and do nice things for you if you will make me feel good in return."

Spiritually and emotionally mature youth leaders meet the needs of teenagers with no thought of reward. Such leaders simply "accept one another, just as Christ also accepted us to the glory of God" (Romans 15:7).

Teenagers who are quiet at church may have personal lives filled with pain and chaos. The key people in their lives may ignore them or continually berate them. When a leader at church gives such a teenager a warm affirmation, that might be the only positive word that teenager receives the entire week. That moment may not seem like much, but for a few teenagers, it might be life-saving.

A day will come when youth leaders will look back on life and wonder what contributions they made for the Kingdom. Everyone wants to know that his life has mattered in some way. Across the years, a genuine ministry to the least-loved and least-attractive will perhaps make a more permanent difference in people's lives than any other.

TRUTH 21

Youth leaders guide teenagers to invite the Holy Spirit to empower their spiritual gifts to serve the King.

Teenage believers are the church today as well as the church tomorrow. Full entrance into the life of the church is a privilege open to all baptized believers. There is no Scriptural basis for delaying full churchmanship to some predetermined age.

Many teenagers become adults and then die of old age without ever realizing the gifts God had placed within them. This situation is a great loss to the church and the Kingdom.

To be the church today, teenagers must know their spiritual gifts, and they must invite the Holy Spirit to empower those gifts to impact the Kingdom for the glory of God. To that end, the role of youth leaders and parents is crucial. The great majority of teenagers need guidance in "unwrapping the graveclothes" in which their gifts are wrapped.

Paul explained the nature of the spiritual gifts and their distribution, saying, "To each one is given the manifestation of the Spirit for the common good" (1 Corinthians 12:7). Paul also said, "But one and the same Spirit works all these things, distributing to each one individually just as He wills" (1 Corinthians 12:11). The Holy Spirit distributes a rich diversity of gifts for the sake of the Kingdom.

Every teenager has at least one spiritual gift, and each teenager is to be a good steward by using his gift to serve through the church. Youth leaders and parents take the lead in this discovery process. Such a ministry follows the example of Christ. Seeing potential in an ADD middle school boy follows in the same tradition as seeing apostolic characteristics in a cursing fisherman.

The affirmation of gifts and abilities is an ideal way to involve fringe teenagers. Saying, "Come, we need you," is more effective than saying, "Come, you will enjoy it."

Being needed is more important than being entertained.

By the hand of God, teenagers can be "strengthened with power through His Spirit in the inner man" (Ephesians 3:16). As a result, King Jesus "is able to do far more abundantly beyond all that we ask or think, according to the power that works within us" (Ephesians 3:20). Peter adds:

> "As each one has received a special gift, employ it in serving one another as good stewards of the manifold grace of God ... so that in all things God may be glorified through Jesus Christ, to whom belongs the glory and dominion forever and ever" (1 Peter 4:10-11).

The Holy Spirit takes the lead role in revealing to teenagers which spiritual gifts they have received. And the Spirit provides the power that allows those gifts to make a supernatural impact. In all this, the Spirit rivets attention on God's mighty Son:

> "But when He, the Spirit of truth, comes, He will guide you into all the truth; for He will not speak on His own initiative, but whatever He hears, He will speak; and He will disclose to you what is to come. He will glorify Me, for He will take of Mine and will disclose it to you" (John 16:13-14).

Youth leaders discern *their* spiritual gifts through the study of Scripture, through the voice of the Holy Spirit, and through the counsel of godly pastors and leaders. Youth leaders then invite the Holy Spirit to empower those gifts to bring in the Kingdom for the glory of God.

Then, youth leaders guide teenagers through a similar process. Spirit-empowered and gifted teenagers then bring in the Kingdom, now and for a lifetime, for the glory of the Almighty.

TRUTH 22

Youth leaders equip teenagers to do what King Jesus has called them to do.

God uses youth leaders to equip teenagers for His work—"He gave some as apostles, and some as prophets, and some as evangelists, and some as pastors and *teachers*, for the *equipping* of the saints for the work of service, to the building up of the body of Christ" (Ephesians 4:11-12, emphasis added). A few parents might disagree, but teenagers are among the saints of God.

Youth leaders use the Bible as the primary textbook to equip teenagers. As Paul wrote to young Timothy, "All Scripture is inspired by God and profitable for teaching, for reproof, for correction, for *training* in righteousness; so that the man of God may be adequate, *equipped* for every good work" (2 Timothy 3:16-17, emphasis added). Paul knew that if Timothy were well-grounded in the Scriptures, he would be fully prepared for whatever God called him to do.

Youth leaders help teenagers to understand their place in God's plan and train them to do what He has called them to do. Wise youth leaders discover their plan for equipping by watching Jesus equip His disciples in the Scriptures.

1. The first thing Jesus did was model for the disciples what He wanted them to do. Jesus did the work, and the disciples watched. Jesus preached, taught, and healed under the watchful eye of His new followers.

    As youth leaders model doing God's work, teenagers can learn by watching them. Paul said to the Corinthians, "Be imitators of me, just as I also am of Christ" (1 Corinthians 11:1). This principle might cause a youth leader to ask, "How can I allow teenagers to observe what I do for the Kingdom,

45

either as a group or one-on-one?"

2. Second, Jesus did the work while the disciples assisted. In Mark 6, Jesus performed a miracle by feeding 5,000 people. The disciples joined Jesus in this ministry by feeding the multitude—"He blessed the food and broke the loaves and He kept giving them to the disciples to set before them" (Mark 6:41).

   Teenage believers need to assist in the work of the Kingdom. Teenagers need opportunities to serve in all the varied ministries of the church. Teenagers need to serve alongside youth leaders and other adults of the church to learn how the work is done firsthand.

3. Third, the disciples did the work, and Jesus assisted them. After the transfiguration, the disciples were asked to cast out a demon from a possessed boy. When they were unsuccessful, the frustrated father of the boy asked Jesus to intervene. Jesus used this failure to teach the disciples—"'Why could we not drive it out?' And He said to them, 'This kind cannot come out by anything but prayer'" (Mark 9:28-29).

4. Fourth, the disciples did the work, and Jesus watched. In Luke 10, Jesus sent the disciples out to heal the sick and proclaim the Kingdom of God. When the disciples returned, they reported to Jesus, "Lord, even the demons are subject to us in Your name" (Luke 10:17). Jesus gave them instructions, they went out and performed the work, and they came back joyfully because the work was successful.

5. Finally, Jesus unleashed the disciples to take on the specific ministries He had crafted for them. Jesus modeled, equipped, and encouraged the disciples to change the world.

If equipping the disciples was important to Him, then equipping teenagers should be important to youth leaders. To what end? To glorify the King who is ascended, anointed, and crowned as supreme in all things—filling the universe with His sovereignty, majesty, activity, and presence!

TRUTH 23

Youth leaders guide teenagers to follow God's call to a vocation.

Teenage disciples seek God's unique will in a vocation, follow Him where He leads, and then perform their occupation in a way that brings in His Kingdom for His glory. They view every vocation as a ministry.

In the Old Testament, ministry was largely the responsibility of the few, the priesthood. In the New Testament, all true believers are priests, and thus the ministry is the work of all the saints. Peter wrote:

> "You are a chosen race, a royal priesthood, a holy nation, a people for God's own possession, so that you may proclaim the excellencies of Him who has called you out of darkness into His marvelous light" (1 Peter 2:9).

Every teenager (and every believer) is called to the ministry. Ministry isn't a career, but a lifestyle. To minister is to serve, a calling common to all Christians. Jesus Himself "did not come to be served, but to serve" (Mark 10:45).

"'Vocation' comes from the Latin verb *vocare*, which means 'to call.' ... The definition suggests that a person listens for something which calls out to him. The calling is something which comes to someone and is particular to someone."[41]

Some use the term *vocational ministry* to refer to the work done by a person who makes his or her living through some type of church-related work. In reality, all believers have a type of vocational ministry. That vocation may or may not contribute to their finances, and it may or may not be immediately recognizable as "Christian."

Today, drawing a sharp line between "secular" and "religious" vocations is difficult. For example, someone might teach school full-time to serve a small church as youth pastor without salary. Overseas, some might work in business or finance so they can spend their evenings and weekends planting churches. Or someone might teach science in a public high school to reveal God's creative genius to the students as pre-evangelism.

For those serving in each of these ways, Paul would say, "As the Lord has assigned to each one, as God has called each, in this manner let him walk" (1 Corinthians 7:17). Vocation thus becomes a way of fulfilling one's calling in Hollywood, on Wall Street, in the courthouse, or on the job site.

At the same time, God calls some teenagers to earn their income by serving a church, missions agency, or ministry organization:

> "The elders who rule well are to be considered worthy of double honor, especially those who work hard at preaching and teaching. For the Scripture says, 'You shall not muzzle the ox while he is threshing,' and 'The laborer is worthy of his wages'" (1 Timothy 5:17-18).

Youth leaders have much to offer related to vocation. What they do (or don't do) will help determine the quality of the environment out of which teenagers hear God's voice related to vocations.

You can share with teenagers your answers to questions such as these:

- "What is your sense of calling through your vocation?"
- "How did Christ direct you to what you are doing?"
- "How is Christ bringing in His Kingdom through your vocation?"

Youth leaders can let teenagers know about opportunities in ministry vocations. Teenagers are not likely to feel called to an area of service they don't even know exists. Knowledge of opportunities does not produce a call, but it does precede a call. Options open today go far beyond being a preacher or missionary.

Every teenager (and every youth leader) can seek God's unique will, follow Him where He leads, and then perform one's occupation in a way that brings in His Kingdom for the honor and glory of the Regal One.

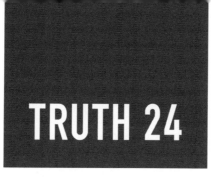

TRUTH 24

Youth leaders prepare teenagers for major life decisions.

No spiritually sensitive youth leader can turn off concern for a teenager the night of high school graduation. Instead, that leader will ask, "Will the spiritual investment in this person lead to a life that brings joy to God and impact for His Kingdom? Will this new graduate make major life decisions that flow out of a delight in King Jesus?"

Youth leaders cooperate with the Spirit in guiding young believers in making major decisions while they are teenagers. At the same time, discovering the will of God is a lifetime process.

Teenagers need to say, "My leaders helped me make an important decision while I was in high school." But it is even more important for teenagers to say, "My leaders taught me how to find God's will in decisions for the rest of my life."

Youth leaders need to guide teenagers to live in the center of God's will today. Some teenagers anxious to know God's answers for the future are unconcerned about living for Him in the present. They need to know that walking in His will today is very much related to finding His plans for the future:

> "Trust in the Lord with all your heart and do not lean on your own understanding. *In all your ways acknowledge Him*, and He will make your paths straight" (Proverbs 3:5-6, emphasis added).

Youth leaders need to guide teenagers to use the Bible to discern God's will. General principles of Scripture apply to every life situation. Specific instructions relate to many future decisions. Most of what King Jesus wants teenagers to know about His way He has already revealed in the Bible.

Youth leaders need to guide teenagers to live in grace and forgiveness. Unresolved guilt can become a hairball that stops up the conduit between a young believer and the Almighty. "I'm not sure we understand how much of our ongoing sin hinders our following God faithfully. ... Moreover, it makes it difficult to hear God clearly."[42]

Youth leaders need to guide teenagers to make every decision in light of the supreme majesty of God's beloved Son:

> Christians believe in Jesus Christ not only because we see him ascended and active as Lord of all, but also because we see everything else in the universe as it really is through the lens of his spectacular supremacy.[43]

Thus, the primary question in choosing a marriage partner never is, "Will I be happy?" The primary question in choosing a vocation never is, "Will I find this job rewarding, and will I make lots of money?" The primary question in considering a career move never is, "Will this make me more famous and give me more influence?"

Instead, the primary questions are:

- Is this choice consistent with the full counsel of the Bible, properly interpreted?
- Is this choice consistent with the leadership of the Holy Spirit when I listen to Him most carefully?
- Is this the choice that will bring the greatest honor and glory to King Jesus?
- Is this the choice that will best allow me to join my King in bringing His Kingdom on earth?

But here is a paradox. When teenage believers take their eyes off of self and choose to live for the glory of Christ—when they make His Kingdom paramount in their decisions—then something unexpected happens:

> "Delight yourself in the Lord; and He will give
> you the desires of your heart" (Psalm 37:4).
> What a glorious King!

TRUTH 25

Youth leaders guide parents and the congregation to form heart connections with teenagers.

A heart connection is a pipeline that connects the heart of a teenager and another believer. Through that pipeline, spiritual impact flows from one person or one generation to the next. Teenagers experience transformation, in part, through warm heart connections with parents, youth leaders, peers, and members of the congregation.

Parents who keep heart connections warm and strong usually see visible evidence that their faith and values are passing to their children. "And he will turn the hearts of fathers to their children and the hearts of children to their fathers" (Malachi 4:6, ESV). Teenagers who are loved by their parents with the warm love of Christ more easily embrace Christ Himself.

Teenagers tend to share strong heart connections with parents who communicate their significance and frequently provide words of encouragement. "Do not let any unwholesome talk come out of your mouths, but only what is helpful for building others up according to their needs, that it may benefit those who listen" (Ephesians 4:29, NIV).

Teenagers tend to share strong heart connections with parents who spend focused time with them. Young believers don't impact the Kingdom because they go to better schools, wear the proper labels, or have more elaborate vacations. They become emotionally and spiritually vibrant young adults because, in part, they spend powerful hours receiving the attention of their parents.

On the other hand, too little quality time together or emotional injury can damage heart connections. Parents with damaged heart connections have little spiritual impact—even if they teach and live out biblical truth before their teenagers. "Truth without relationship leads to rejection. We are losing our kids not because they don't hear the truth, but because the people speaking the truth haven't spent the time to build relationships with them."[44]

Parents rebuild heart connections by forgiving teenagers for the pain they have caused, by asking them for forgiveness as appropriate, by moving away from emotional outbursts toward teenagers, by giving focused attention, and by using words to bless, encourage, and build up.

Teenagers experience transformation, in part, through warm heart connections with youth leaders. Youth leaders build heart connections with teenagers much the same way as parents do—by offering unconditional love, using words that encourage and build up, and spending focused time with them. In the absence of heart connections, even well-planned lessons contribute little to lifetime faith.

Teenagers experience transformation, in part, through warm heart connections with peers. Leaders teach principles from Scripture that motivate and equip teenagers to give and receive unfailing love, encouragement, and focused attention. Leaders then create activities and environments most likely to connect the hearts of youth group members. What some observers consider wasted fun time actually prompts sanctification *through* peers who "stimulate one another to love and good deeds" (Hebrews 10:24).

Teenagers experience transformation, in part, through warm heart connections with members of the congregation. But such connections are rare in most churches since churches typically have segregated teenagers from the congregation for the past 70 years. Left to themselves, neither teenagers nor adults will take the initiative to form heart-level relationships.

Pastors, parents, and youth leaders need to link arms and share biblical truth related to warm relationships among *all* the members of the body of Christ. Then, leaders need to create times and places for the generations to break the ice, begin relationships, and grow true heart connections.

A teenager who graduates high school with rich heart connections with parents, youth leaders, peers, and the congregation almost certainly will spend a lifetime embracing the full supremacy of the Son.

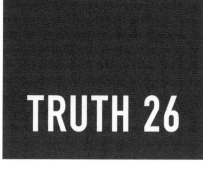

TRUTH 26

Youth leaders guide teenagers to share life and ministry with all the generations of the congregation.

In healthy churches and youth ministries, all the generations come together at times for both worship and discipleship. This type of ministry is evident throughout Scripture. God's people came together often in both the Old and New Testaments for the sake of teaching God's Word to the younger generation and worshiping with one another.

The generations gathered for prayer and confession in Ezra 10:1: "Now while Ezra was praying and making confession, weeping and prostrating himself before the house of God, a very large assembly, men, women and children, gathered...."

A similar ministry took place in Joshua 8 when Joshua renewed the Lord's covenant: "There was not a word of all that Moses had commanded which Joshua did not read before all the assembly of Israel" (Joshua 8:35). This ministry of the Word included "the women and the little ones and the strangers who were living among them."

Nehemiah 8 paints a similar picture. Ezra read the Lord's commands as a multigenerational community of God's people participated in the day of worship. Men, women, and all who could understand were present.

Today's church should be encouraged by these Old Testament examples, for youth ministry is a churchwide ministry. Youth leaders find a strong pattern for this in the New Testament as well.

When Paul wrote Timothy, he called him "my true child in the faith" (1 Timothy 1:2). However, Paul later made clear that others discipled Timothy first. Paul wrote, "I am mindful of the sincere faith within you, which first dwelt in your grandmother Lois and your mother Eunice, and I am sure that it is in you as well" (2 Timothy

1:5). Here, one finds a mother, a grandmother, and a minister all investing in young Timothy's spiritual growth.

God desires for each generation to impact the next generation because the adage is true that:

The church is just one generation away from extinction.

In Judges 2, the author notes Joshua's death and then a sort of spiritual amnesia that arose with the next generation. The heartbreaking words appear in Judges 2:10: "There arose another generation after them who did not know the Lord."

The Israelite families served God as long as Joshua and his elders were alive. When Joshua and his elders died, however, another generation arose. These families "did not know the Lord, nor yet the work which He had done for Israel" (Judges 2:10b).

The unbelief of the new generation is explicit in the next verse as "the sons of Israel did evil in the sight of the Lord and served the Baals, and they forsook the Lord, the God of their fathers, who had brought them out of the land of Egypt" (Judges 2:11-12a).

The opposite can also be true, however. The older generation can have the needed influence on the spiritual lives of teenagers today. Youth leaders can create opportunities for older adults to pass their faith to the next generation, blessing the church with a legacy of faith.

At the same time, generational influence can work both ways. Teenagers need the pragmatism of older adults, but adults need the idealism of teenagers as well. Youthful ideas can help prevent the church's drifting toward self-serving institutionalism. The church needs the balance between teenage and older-adult thinking.

The church needs the excitement and enthusiasm of teenagers. Such excitement should not be reserved for youth activities outside the mainstream of church life. The entire congregation needs to feel the vibrancy of teenagers who are functioning fully as church members.

Teenagers who share life and ministry with all the generations are most likely to
love God
love people
make disciples for a lifetime

TRUTH 27

Youth leaders view teenagers as young adults rather than overgrown children.

Scripture supports the perspective that the ages of approximately 12 to 18 represent a distinct stage of life.[45] Some of the ministry of the church needs to be laser-focused on the unique needs and challenges of those in this distinct stage. But a biblically sound approach will view them as a distinct grouping of very young adults rather than a grouping of leftover children.

Teenagers in the Bible usually functioned as adults and were viewed as adults. Given the practices of the day, the mother of Jesus likely was a younger teenager. The Bible may suggest that 11 of the 12 apostles were older teenagers.[46] King Uzziah, King Josiah, King David, Daniel, Joseph, Samuel, Samson, Esther, and others demonstrated adult maturity in their teenage years.

For most of human history, children learning and working alongside parents and other adults transitioned to adulthood by their early to late teens. In the Middle Ages, adult apprenticeships began as young as 7. Young people married soon after puberty and set up independent households.

At 17, your great-grandfather likely plowed all day behind a mule and then went home to help with the baby. Your great-grandmother worked just as hard and just as competently. At 16 she washed clothes by hand with soap she had made, cooked from a fire she had built, roasted chickens she raised herself, took care of the children, planted her own garden, and still had time to care for her husband. Both performed well in their roles because adults had invested years preparing them for just that.[47]

Many developments led the culture to perceive a new stage of life called "adolescence." That stage of life was the creation of modern industrialization, child labor laws, school systems, and other factors emerging between 1880 and 1920. New laws and cultural practices began to separate teenagers from adults.

For most contemporary adults, the concept of adolescence implies extended childhood, marking time, hanging out, and dwelling in a Neverland between childhood and adulthood. In that regard, the concept of adolescence is not helpful to the Kingdom. The concept impedes families and churches as they seek to rear young adults who are motivated and prepared *now* to fulfill their unique missions on the earth.

For many teenage believers today, their faith is an underdeveloped, "adolescent" faith. Most set this weak faith aside during adulthood. Thus, most are not fulfilling their unique calling and mission on earth and are not bringing glory to God.

Would viewing teenagers as very young adults require a change for your church? For you? Is it time for youth leaders to challenge teenagers to do hard things for the Kingdom? "Life without some sense of urgency—a life that is safe, incubated, insular, overprotected, consumptive—is not worth living. The next generation is aching for influence, for significance, for lives of meaning and impact."[48] A well-known youth ministry speaker reports:

> As I travel the nation, I encounter teenagers everywhere who are sick and tired of typical church and dying instead for authentic Christianity. Students all over the nation are crying out for something real. They want a driving cause to live for, and if necessary, to die for. They are tired of the traditional. They long for the radical.[49]

Bottom line, teenagers in most churches tend to be seriously underchallenged. That is sad because, right now, many teenagers are primed and ready to do hard things, to take on grand challenges. As very young adults, they are ready to join Paul in saying, "For to me, to live is Christ and to die is gain" (Philippians 1:21).

TRUTH 28

Youth leaders guide teenagers to become good stewards of their time, talents, and treasures.

The concrete has already been poured and will begin to harden soon. The stewardship attitudes and lifestyle of teenagers are close to being set for adulthood. Youth leaders and parents will need to move quickly to bring influence to bear on this vital arena of life. A clear understanding of stewardship is the place to begin.

Both the Hebrew term *asher al bayith* and the New Testament Greek word *oikonomia*, which are translated steward, carry the general idea of "one over or in charge of the management of a house." Much of the New Testament's teaching on stewardship is found in Jesus' parables, and the point of the parables is that the steward is accountable to the master for the exercise of his stewardship.[50]

Stewardship refers to more than the use of money. A frequently used definition suggests that Christian stewardship is "the ordering or shaping of the whole of life in accordance with the will of God as revealed in Jesus Christ. This concept of stewardship includes daily activities, goals for living, and the relationships with other people and with material things."[51]

Youth leaders value stewardship because Jesus values stewardship. In the Gospel of Matthew, Jesus told the parable of the talents (see Matthew 25:14-30). Stewardship builds trust. In the parable, the master responded to the good stewards by saying, "You were faithful with a few things, I will put you in charge of many things" (verse 23b). Stewardship leads to joy. The master concludes his praise of the steward by saying, "Enter into the joy of your master" (verse 23c).

- The culture only views life and stewardship from the here and now; Christianity views life from a heavenly perspective.
- The culture views life only from the perspective of material reality; Christianity views life from the perspective of God and His providence.
- The culture lives for today; Christianity lives for today and forever.
- The culture gets for self; Christianity gives of self.
- The culture indulges in luxury; Christianity serves.

The secular world has convinced many church members that some former luxuries are now necessities. Americans are so accustomed to prosperity that they seldom distinguish between their wants and needs.

Youth leaders have the wonderful privilege of serving as role models to teenagers related to stewardship. Young disciples need to see a leader who is voluntarily adopting a simpler lifestyle than his or her salary would permit in order to minister in Christ's name with the surplus. This principle is true regardless of income. Teenagers who do not see such a pattern in the leader's life may be unmoved by lessons on the topic.

Youth leaders also can expose teenagers to other adults who are examples of God's principles of stewardship. In almost every church, a few adults are building their lives around God's values in stewardship. Teenagers need to have close contact with such individuals. They need to see adult disciples who are doing worthwhile things with their time and talents. They need to see adults who are accomplishing good through the responsible use of their possessions.

Even though stewardship training in the church is vitally important, the fact remains that most stewardship values are transmitted in the home. Helping parents to grow in this area may be one of the primary ways to influence the stewardship values of teenagers.

Through every means possible, youth leaders prepare teenagers for total stewardship of life and resources—young disciples able to say, "I count all things to be loss in view of the surpassing value of knowing Christ Jesus my Lord" (Philippians 3:8).

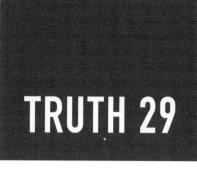

TRUTH 29

Youth leaders guide teenagers to live a lifetime in sexual purity for the glory of King Jesus.

Sex as God created it is one of His most beautiful creations and most wonderful gifts. Sex experienced according to God's design brings joy and ultimately brings glory to Him. Only in disobedience does sex become something less than good. Christ-followers move toward sexual purity in the power of the Spirit.

Many Christian leaders and Bible scholars came together to write summaries of the teaching of Scripture regarding sexual purity. Those helpful summaries include these statements:

We affirm that God has designed marriage to be a covenantal, sexual, procreative, lifelong union of one man and one woman, as husband and wife, and is meant to signify the covenant love between Christ and his bride the church. We deny that God has designed marriage to be a homosexual, polygamous, or polyamorous relationship. We also deny that marriage is a mere human contract rather than a covenant made before God.

We affirm that God's revealed will for all people is chastity outside of marriage and fidelity within marriage. We deny that any affections, desires, or commitments ever justify sexual intercourse before or outside marriage; nor do they justify any form of sexual immorality.[52]

People increasingly think that human identity as male and female is not part of God's beautiful plan but is an expression of an individual's preferences. But the Bible teaches otherwise.

Youth leaders develop teenagers who embrace the gender identity God chose for them at conception. God decides whether teenagers are born male or female. "The gender of each is a form of identity given distinctly to each. The gifts of maleness and femaleness are not in the power of humanity, but in the gift of God."[53]

Teenagers need to know that the heart is the command center of human life. It controls everything a person does. "In essence, all sinful actions are an overflow of the heart, and in order to experience change in behavior, a genuine heart change is first needed. ... If we only try to correct the behavior, we will never succeed since the problem lies within the heart."[54] Leaders say to teenagers:

> You need to realize that you really don't have a lust problem, a sex problem, a pornographic problem, or a behavioral problem. What you really have is a heart problem. The good news is that the power of the gospel can change our sick, deceitful hearts and make them brand new. Jesus is the cure for your heart problem.[55]

King Jesus transforms hearts through grace and forgiveness. Youth leaders invite teenagers to receive God's forgiveness for the mistakes they have made. "When we confess our sin to God, we are ... admitting to and agreeing with God that we are imperfect and sinful. To repent simply means to turn away and turn around."[56] And leaders remind teenagers that they may need to forgive others for the sins they committed against them.

Teenagers with cleansed and transformed hearts increasingly should be able to say: "My purity is for His delight primarily. If I should be single all my life, my heart will be full of joy over the relationship I have shared with my regal King, thankful that immorality never harmed the depth of intimacy we have shared. As my King Regent, He has every right to all of me—including the sexual me. I am His alone. He is the main thing, the only thing that matters ultimately. I am waiting for unimaginable closeness with Him in heaven. And I want nothing on earth that impinges on my delight in Him forever."

TRUTH 30

Youth leaders experience occasional disappointment and find a God who is sufficient.

Many youth leaders go through periods when they are almost discouraged enough to quit. In fact, many do leave youth ministry every year. However, there are certainly some positive alternatives to leaving the work to which one has been called.

King Jesus is sufficient to meet all the needs of youth leaders in the midst of the most difficult days of life. His Word has wisdom in how to view those experiences—"Consider it all joy, my brethren, when you encounter various trials, knowing that the testing of your faith produces endurance. And let endurance have its perfect result, so that you may be perfect and complete, lacking in nothing" (James 1:2-4).

A youth leader in the middle of a church split would not automatically view that experience as a "friend." Neither would a leader discouraged by an unresponsive Bible class. But Scripture is correct. Leaders can see difficult experiences in a positive light because of what God can accomplish in the life of a leader *through* those experiences.

God allows adversity. Viewing a difficult situation as an opportunity for God to deepen character and to teach endurance can create a much more positive mind-set.

A number of situations can be discouraging to a youth leader.

1. *Mistakes*—Making errors, especially public ones, can be discouraging. But God is sufficient. He is the only one to whom leaders can commit mistakes. He knows His children, and He accepts them just as they are. Even on the darkest days, leaders do not need to fear His rejection.

2. *Misunderstandings*—Being misunderstood hurts. When someone takes offense at an innocent act, a youth leader may come away emotionally drained.

> But when you give the situation over to God and say—"Lord, I am defenseless. I am misunderstood. I am right, but they'll never believe it. You take over"—God will perform the most unbelievable feats as He glorifies His name in your life. That's His specialty![57]

3. *Feeling inferior*—Almost every leader is tempted to equate his or her worth as an individual with "success" in leading teenagers. Comparing one's ministry to other leaders can leave someone with few feelings of self-worth. Again, God has the answer. He reminds a leader that, even before birth, he or she was designed for a special purpose. Part of that creative process still is underway and should not be judged too early. God wants all eyes on Him, not on the youth ministry superstars leaders never were supposed to be.

The biblical concept of hope is powerful as it calls believers to look beyond present circumstances and to fix their eyes on all that is awaiting them in the Kingdom of God:

> "We exult in *hope* of the glory of God. And not only this, but we also exult in our tribulations, knowing that tribulation brings about perseverance; and perseverance, proven character; and proven character, *hope*; and *hope* does not disappoint, because the love of God has been poured out within our hearts through the Holy Spirit who was given to us" (Romans 5:2b-5, emphasis added).

Teenagers filled with biblical hope can battle their daily challenges with confidence. Then, they need to watch youth leaders who face their own challenges with confidence because they have riveted their eyes on King Jesus.

TRUTH 31

Youth leaders invite teenagers to make leisure time and recreation elements of abundant living.

Jesus smiles when His young disciples take the Gospel to an unreached group. Jesus smiles when His young disciples help dig a water well in an arid land. But does Jesus also smile when His teenagers enjoy playing a great game? Here is a hint: Jesus is the One who said, "I came that they may have life, and have it abundantly" (John 10:10b). He also led Paul to name "joy" as a fruit of the Spirit (see Galatians 5:22-23).

A few youth leaders have moved completely away from "all that fun and games stuff." Those leaders say things like: "I felt I had more to offer than pizza and sodas." "I got tired of feeling like a babysitter." "It is more important to see teenagers praying than playing."

An earlier era of youth ministry did feature too much time in the fun-and-games department. Movement away from that overbalance was wise. But now it would be unwise to throw the proverbial baby out with the bathwater. When properly balanced with the other elements of youth ministry, recreation and leisure time do have contributions to make. In fact, they serve and support other elements of ministry:

1. Recreation allows the church to minister to the whole teenager.
2. Recreation is a tool for reaching teenagers and drawing them into youth ministry.
3. Recreation prepares teenagers to use leisure time as adults.
4. Recreation develops the creativity of teenagers.
5. Recreation strengthens how teenagers see themselves as it gives them success experiences.

6. Recreation breaks down social and economic barriers in the church and youth group.
7. Recreation strengthens families through activities that stimulate family togetherness, teamwork, and shared leisure time.[58]

Teenage believers need a peer group that supports their faith and daily walk. Recreation is an important tool to use in building supportive peer groups around each teenager. Without any recreation, a youth group may be little more than a collection of individuals.

As in most other areas of youth ministry, leadership is the key in recreation. Teachers, leaders, and coaches who are Christlike, loving, affirming, and challenging can use recreation to accomplish many important goals with teenagers.

Conclusion

Thirty-one truths to shape your youth ministry. All focused on seeing teenagers who, for the glory of the Father and in the power of the Spirit, spend a lifetime embracing the full supremacy of the Son, responding to His majesty in all of life, inviting Christ to live His life through them, and joining Him in making disciples among all peoples.

Come upon us, Lord Jesus Christ!
Break in and break through upon us without delay!
Answer this cry in ways
That approximate how one day—one grand and glorious day—
Your triumphs will be displayed
Throughout all heaven and earth,
Bringing everlasting praise to our triune God.
Between this day and that day
Never stop coming down upon us!
Come in the fullness of your spectacular supremacy!
Come in the fervor of your magnificent majesty!
Son of the Father,
Focus of the Spirit,
Hymn of the angels,
Ruler of the nations,
Redeemer of the Church!
Our. Lord. Jesus. Christ.
COME![59]

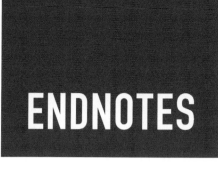

ENDNOTES

Truth 1
[1]David Bryant, *Christ Is Now!* (New Providence, NJ: New Providence Publishers, 2017).

Truth 2
[2]Bryant, *Christ Is Now!*, 155.

Truth 3
[3]Bryant, *Christ Is Now!*, 571.

Truth 7
[4]Bryant, *Christ Is Now!*, 592.

[5]Ibid.

Truth 8
[6]Darren DePaul, "Making Disciples Who Make Disciples" in *Gospel-Centered Youth Ministry*, Cameron Cole and Jon Nielson, eds. (Wheaton, IL: Crossway, 2016), 40.

Truth 9
[7]Bryant, *Christ Is Now!*, 97.

[8]Matt Carter and Josh Wredberg, *Christ-Centered Exposition: Exalting Jesus in John* (Nashville, TN: B&H Publishing Group, 2017), 278.

[9]Philip Walkley and Drew Haltom, "Bearing Gospel Fruit among the Poor" in *Gospel-Centered Youth Ministry*, Cameron Cole and Jon Nielson, eds. (Wheaton, IL: Crossway Publishers, 2016), 180.

[10]Greg Stier, *Gospelize Your Youth Ministry* (Arvada, CO: Dare 2 Share, 2015), 182.

[11]Francis Chan, *Crazy Love* (Colorado Springs: David C. Cook Publishers, 2008), 117.

Truth 10
[12]Bryant, *Christ Is Now!*, 27.

[13]Ibid., 144.

Truth 12
[14]J.D. Greear, *Gospel: Recovering the Power that Made Christianity Revolutionary* (Nashville: B&H Publishing Group, 2011), 14.

[15]Aaron Armstrong, "Crushing the Lie of Moralism," *Facts and Trends*, Spring 2018, accessed June 25, 2018, https://factsandtrends. net/2018/04/11/crushing-the-lie-of-moralism.

[16]Greear, *Gospel*, 46–47.

[17]Bryant, *Christ Is Now!*, 198.

[18]Ibid., 239.

Truth 14
[19]Bryant, *Christ is Now!*, 572.

Truth 15
[20]Duffy Robbins, *Building a Youth Ministry That Builds Disciples* (Grand Rapids, MI: Zondervan, 2011), 77.

[21]Barry Sneed and Roy Edgemon, *Transformational Discipleship* (Nashville: LifeWay, 1999), 3.

[22]Robby Gallaty, *Growing Up: How to Be a Disciple Who Makes Disciples* (Bloomington, IN: CrossBooks, 2013), 19.

[23]David Platt, "Foreword" in *Growing Up*, Gallaty, xvi.

[24]Bryant, *Christ Is Now!*, 572.

[25]Ibid.

Truth 16
[26]John MacArthur, *Unleashing God's Word in Your Life* (Nashville: Thomas Nelson, 2003), 109.

[27]Knute Larson, *Holman New Testament Commentary: I & II Thessalonians, I & II Timothy, Titus, Philemon* (Nashville: B&H Publishers, 2000), 306.

[28]Bryant, *Christ Is Now!*, 397.

Truth 17
[29]Christian Smith, *Soul Searching: The Religious and Spiritual Lives of American Teenagers* (New York: Oxford University Press, 2005), 133.

Truth 18
[30]Dallas Willard, *Renovation of the Heart: Putting on the Character of Christ* (Colorado Springs, CO: NavPress, 2002), 14.

[31]Ibid., 22.

[32]Ibid.

[33]Ibid., 25.

Truth 19
[34]Kara Powell, Brad Griffin, and Cheryl Crawford, *Sticky Faith* (Grand Rapids, MI: Zondervan, 2011), 143.

[35]David Kinnaman, *You Lost Me* (Grand Rapids, MI: Baker Publishing, 2011), 192–93.

[36]Dallas Willard, *The Divine Conspiracy: Rediscovering Our Hidden Life in God* (New York: HarperCollins, 1998), 328.

[37]Ibid.

[38]Derek Rishmawy, "'Who Are You Sleeping With?' My Conversation with Timothy Keller," Patheos, April 11, 2013, accessed June 30, 2018, http://www.patheos.com/blogs/ christandpopculture/2013/04/who-are-you-sleeping-with-my-conversation-with-timothy-keller.

[39]Powell, Griffin, and Crawford, *Sticky Faith*, 143.

[40]Bryant, *Christ Is Now!*, 265–66.

Truth 23
[41]Hugh Whelchel, "The Difference between Calling and Work," Bible.org, accessed July 4, 2018, https://tifwe.org/the-difference-between-calling-and-work.

Truth 24
[42]Chuck Lawless, "Seven Steps When Seeking God's Will," *Southern Baptist Texan* (July 2018), 4.

[43]Bryant, *Christ Is Now!*, 30.

Truth 25
[44]Josh McDowell, "It's Almost Too Late," *New Man Magazine* (June 2003): 56.

Truth 27
[45]See chapter 4 of Richard Ross, *Youth Ministry That Lasts a Lifetime* (Fort Worth: Seminary Hill Press, 2017).

[46]Matthew 17 may suggest only Peter and Jesus owed the temple tax, due from those 21 and older, thus excluding the other 11 apostles.

[47]Johnny Derouen, "The Concept of Adolescence," in Richard Ross, *Accelerate: Parenting Teenagers toward Adulthood* (Nashville: LifeWay, 2015), 9.

[48]Kinnaman, *You Lost Me*, 106.

[49]Greg Stier, *Outbreak: Creating Contagious Youth Ministry through Viral Evangelism* (Chicago: Moody, 2002), 21.

Truth 28
[50]Cecil A. Ray, *How to Specialize in Christian Living* (Nashville: Convention Press, 1981), 44.

[51]Ibid.

Truth 29
[52]Council on Biblical Manhood and Womanhood, "Nashville Statement," https://cbmw.org/wp-content/uploads/2017/08/The-Nashville-Statement.pdf, accessed July 10, 2018, 2.

The statements are drawn from Genesis 1:26–28; 2:15–25; 3:1–24; Exodus 20:14, 17; Leviticus 18:22; 20:13; Deuteronomy 5:18, 21; 22:5; Judges 19:22; 2 Samuel 11:1–12:15; Job 31:1; Psalm 51:1–19; Proverbs 5:1–23; 6:20–35; 7:1–27; Isaiah 59:1; Malachi 2:14; Matthew 5:27–30; 19:4–6, 8–9, 12; Acts 15:20, 29; Romans 1:26–27, 32; 1 Corinthians 6:9–11, 18–20; 7:1–7; 2 Corinthians 5:17; Galatians 5:24; Ephesians 4:15, 20–24; 5:31–32; Colossians 3:5; 1 Thessalonians 4:3–8; 1 Timothy 1:9–10, 15; 2 Timothy 2:22; Titus 2:11–12; Hebrews 13:4; James 1:14–15; 1 Peter 2:11; Jude 7.

[53]Malcolm Yarnell, "A Biblical Anthropology" in Richard Ross, *Youth Ministry That Lasts a Lifetime* (Fort Worth: Seminary Hill Press, 2017), 34.

[54]Clayton King and Sharie King, *True Love Project: Leader Edition* (Nashville: LifeWay Press, 2013), 28.

[55]Ibid., 30.

[56]Ibid., 36.

Truth 30
[57]Charles Swindoll, *Three Steps Forward, Two Steps Back* (Nashville: Thomas Nelson, 1980), 33.

Truth 31
[58]Adapted from Don Mattingly, "Everybody Wins, Nobody Loses!" in *The Complete Youth Ministries Handbook*, Vol. 1, ed. J. David Stone (Nashville: Abingdon, 1970), 196–98.

[59]Bryant, *Christ Is Now!*, 517–19.

BIBLIOGRAPHY

Armstrong, Aaron. "Crushing the Lie of Moralism." *Facts and Trends*. Spring 2018. FactsandTrends.net.

Bryant, David. *Christ Is Now!* New Providence, NJ: New Providence Publishers, 2017.

Carter, Matt and Josh Wredberg. *Christ-Centered Exposition: Exalting Jesus in John*. Nashville, TN: B&H Publishing Group, 2017.

Chan, Francis. *Crazy Love*. Colorado Springs: David C. Cook Publishers, 2008.

Council on Biblical Manhood and Womanhood, "Nashville Statement," https://cbmw.org, accessed July 10, 2018.

DePaul, Darren. "Making Disciples Who Make Disciples" in *Gospel-Centered Youth Ministry*. Cameron Cole and Jon Nielson, eds. Wheaton, IL: Crossway, 2016.

Derouen, Johnny. "The Concept of Adolescence," in Richard Ross. *Accelerate: Parenting Teenagers toward Adulthood*. Nashville: LifeWay, 2015.

Gallaty, Robby. *Growing Up: How to Be a Disciple Who Makes Disciples*. Bloomington, IN: CrossBooks, 2013.

Greear, J.D. *Gospel: Recovering the Power that Made Christianity Revolutionary*. Nashville: B&H Publishing Group, 2011.

Keller, Timothy. *Counterfeit Gods.* New York: Riverhead Books, 2009.

Kinnaman, David. *You Lost Me.* Grand Rapids, MI: Baker, 2011.

Larson, Knute. *Holman New Testament Commentary: I & II Thessalonians, I & II Timothy, Titus, Philemon.* Nashville: B&H Publishers, 2000.

Lawless, Chuck. "Seven Steps When Seeking God's Will." *Southern Baptist Texan.* July 2018.

MacArthur, John. *Unleashing God's Word in Your Life.* Nashville: Thomas Nelson, 2003.

Mattingly, Don. "Everybody Wins, Nobody Loses!" in *The Complete Youth Ministries Handbook.* Vol. 1. J. David Stone, ed. Nashville: Abingdon, 1970.

McDowell, Josh. "It's Almost Too Late." *New Man Magazine.* June 2003.

Platt, David. "Foreword" in Robby Gallaty. *Growing Up: How to Be a Disciple Who Makes Disciples.* Bloomington, IN: CrossBooks, 2013.

Powell, Kara, Brad Griffin, and Cheryl Crawford. *Sticky Faith.* Grand Rapids, MI: Zondervan, 2011.

Ray, Cecil A. *How to Specialize in Christian Living.* Nashville: Convention Press, 1981.

Rishmawy, Derek. "'Who Are You Sleeping With?' My Conversation with Timothy Keller." patheos.com, April 11, 2013.

Robbins, Duffy. *Building a Youth Ministry That Builds Disciples.* Grand Rapids, MI: Zondervan, 2011.

Ross, Richard. *Youth Ministry That Lasts a Lifetime*. Fort Worth: Seminary Hill Press, 2017.

Smith, Christian. *Soul Searching: The Religious and Spiritual Lives of American Teenagers*. New York: Oxford University Press, 2005.

Sneed, Barry and Roy Edgemon. *Transformational Discipleship*. Nashville: LifeWay, 1999.

Stier, Greg. *Gospelize Your Youth Ministry*. Arvada, CO: Dare 2 Share, 2015.

_____. *Outbreak: Creating Contagious Youth Ministry through Viral Evangelism*. Chicago: Moody, 2002.

Swindoll, Charles. *Three Steps Forward, Two Steps Back*. Nashville: Thomas Nelson, 1980.

Walkley, Philip and Drew Haltom. "Bearing Gospel Fruit among the Poor" in *Gospel-Centered Youth Ministry*. Cameron Cole and Jon Nielson, eds. Wheaton, IL: Crossway Publishers, 2016.

Whelchel, Hugh. "The Difference between Calling and Work." Bible.org, accessed July 4, 2018.

Willard, Dallas. *The Divine Conspiracy: Rediscovering Our Hidden Life in God*. New York: HarperCollins, 1998.

_____. *Renovation of the Heart: Putting on the Character of Christ*. Colorado Springs, CO: NavPress, 2002.

Yarnell, Malcolm. "A Biblical Anthropology" in Richard Ross, *Youth Ministry That Lasts a Lifetime*. Fort Worth: Seminary Hill Press, 2017.